Zen Reverie

Finding Peace and Purpose in the QUOTES of Tao

50 Coloring Pages for Harmony, Balance, and Tranquility

Copyright ©2023 All rights reserved.
No part of this publication may be reproduced, stored in a retrieval system, or transmitted in any form or by any means, electronic, mechanical, photocopying, recording, or otherwise, without the prior written permission of the publisher and author, except in the case of brief quotations embodied in critical reviews and certain other noncommercial uses permitted by copyright law.

Test Your Colours Here

If you do not change direction, you may end up where you are heading.

BY LETTING go it all GETS DONE

To a mind that is still the whole Universe surrenders

Accomplish but Do not boast

ACCOMPLISH WITHOUT ARROGANCE

Accomplish without Grabbing

The further one goes, the less one knows.

Loss is not as bad as wanting more.

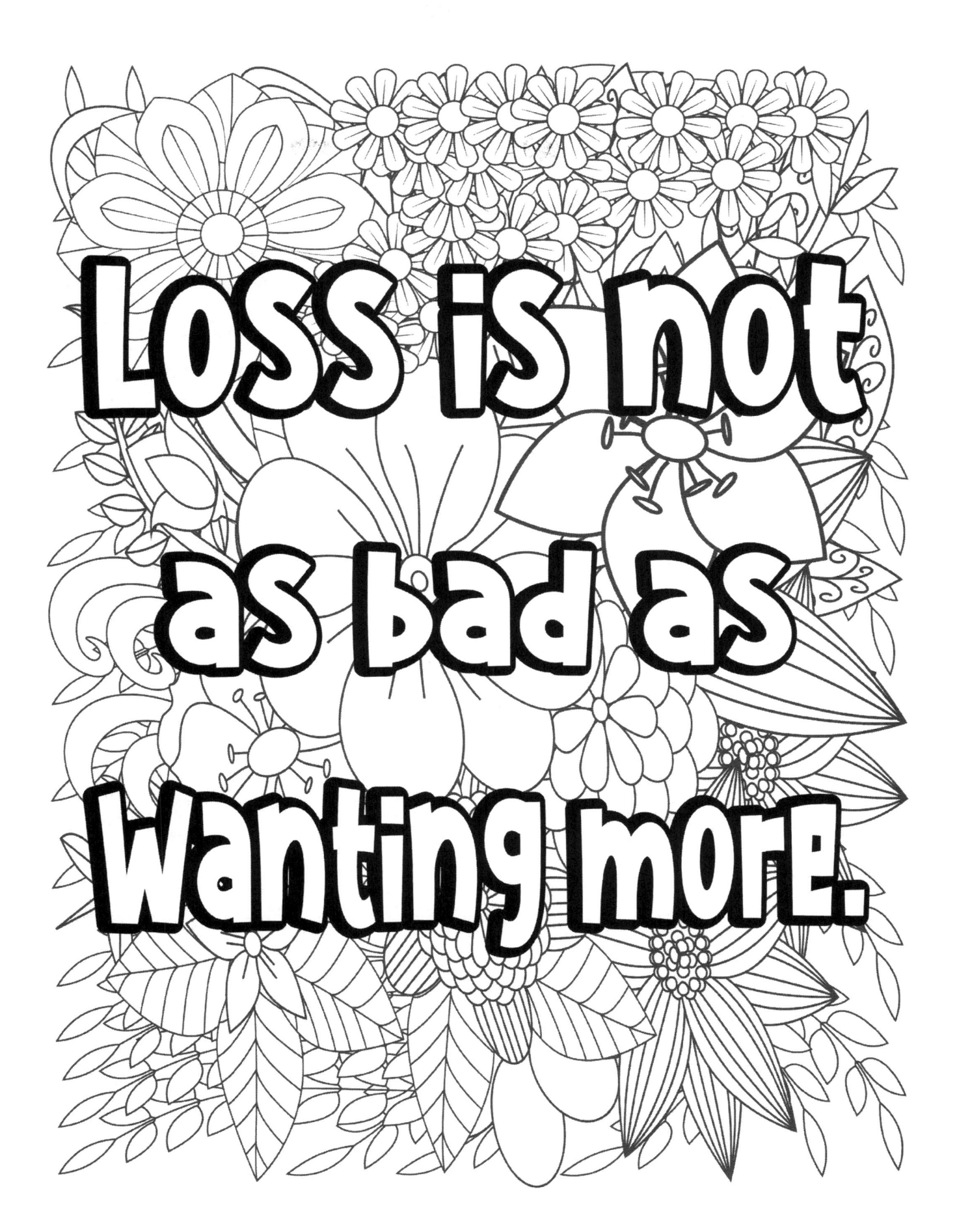

MUDDY WATER, let stand, BECOMES CLEAR

The way to do is to be.

Because of a *great love,* One is courageous.

Perfection is the willingness to be imperfect.

Great acts are made up of small deeds.

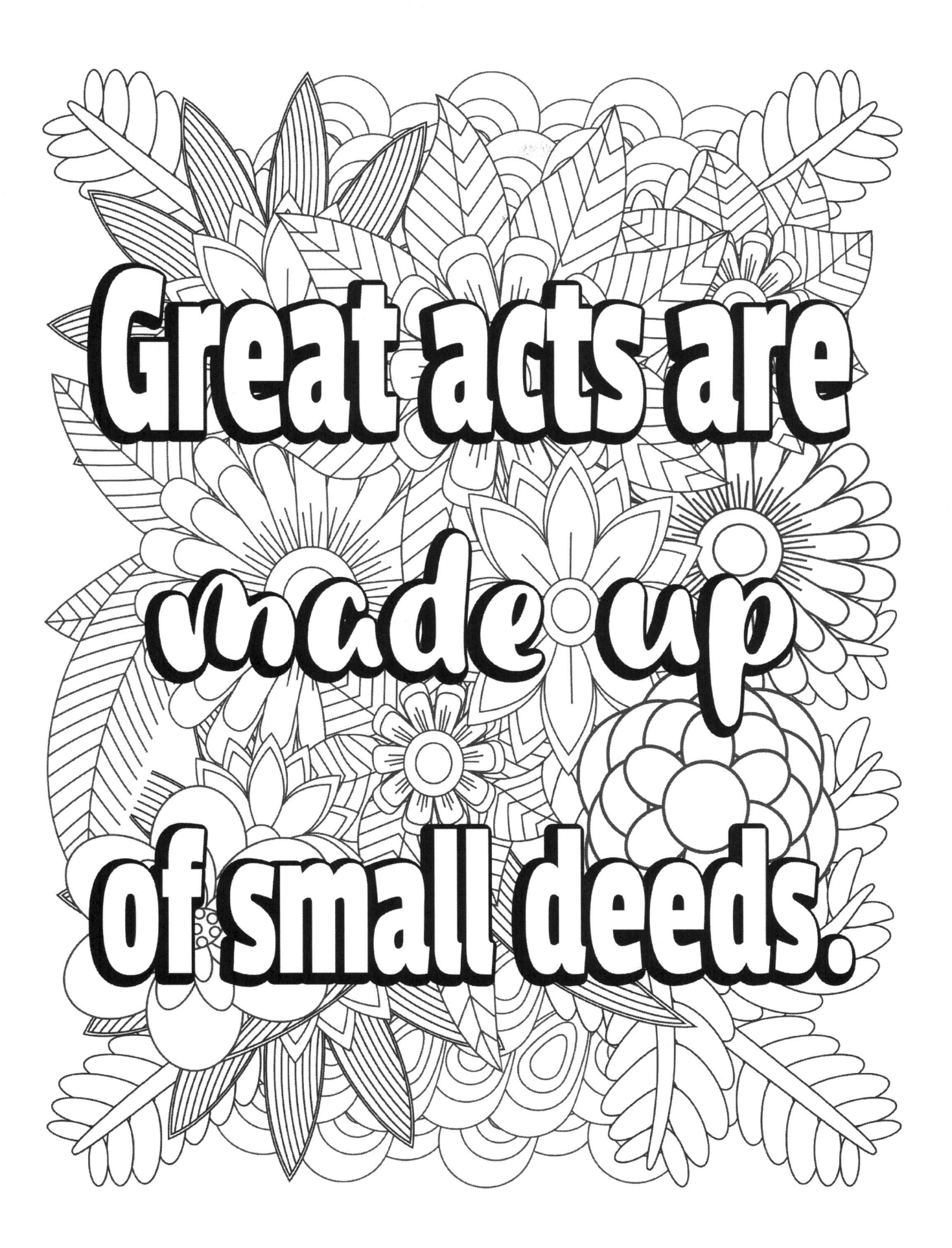

Be still, stillness reveals the secrets eternity

There is no illusion greater than fear

Take care with the end As you do with the beginning

Be like water

THE JOURNEY OF A THOUSAND MILES BEGINS WITH A SINGLE STEP

The heart that gives, Gathers.

Knowing how to yield is Strength

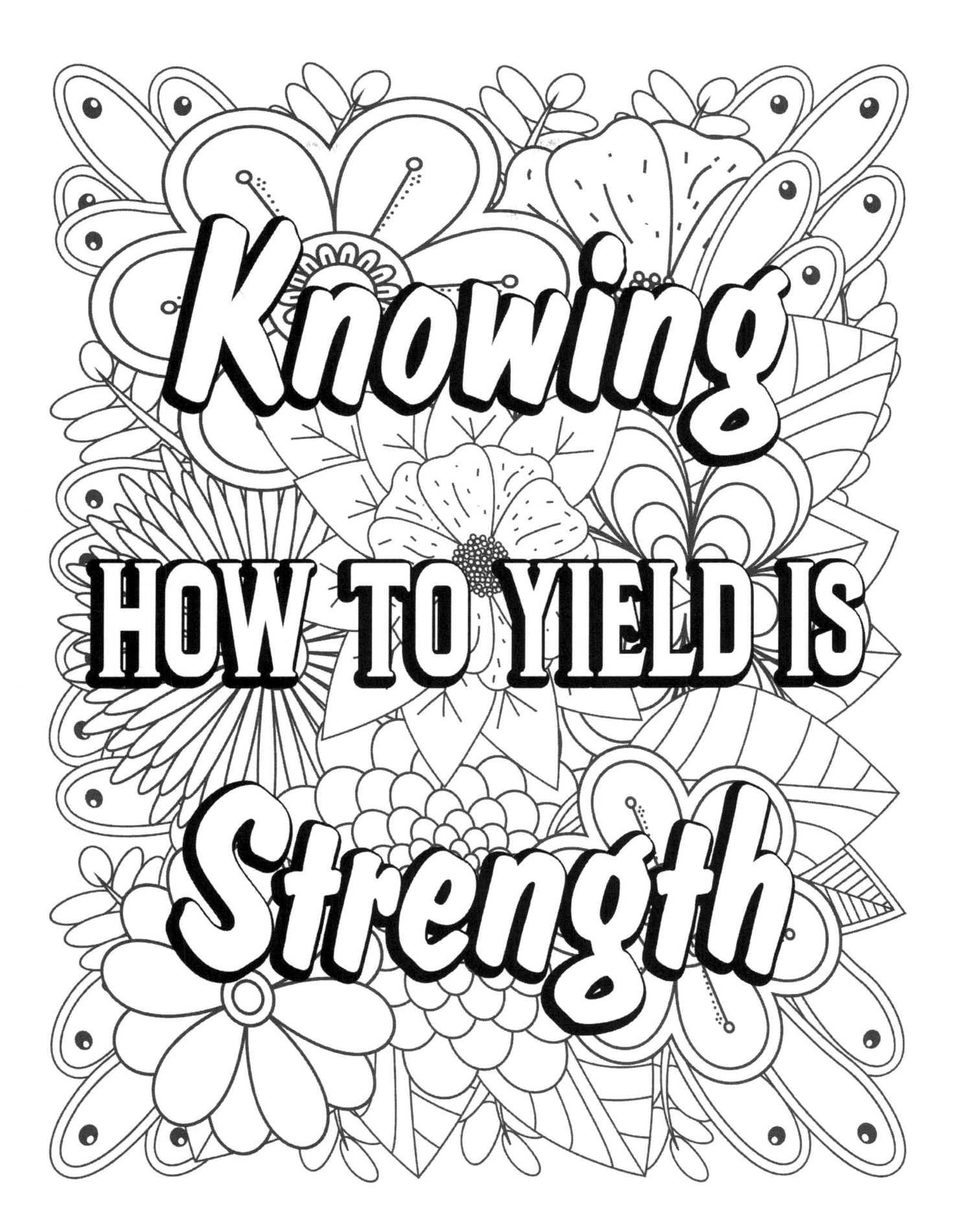

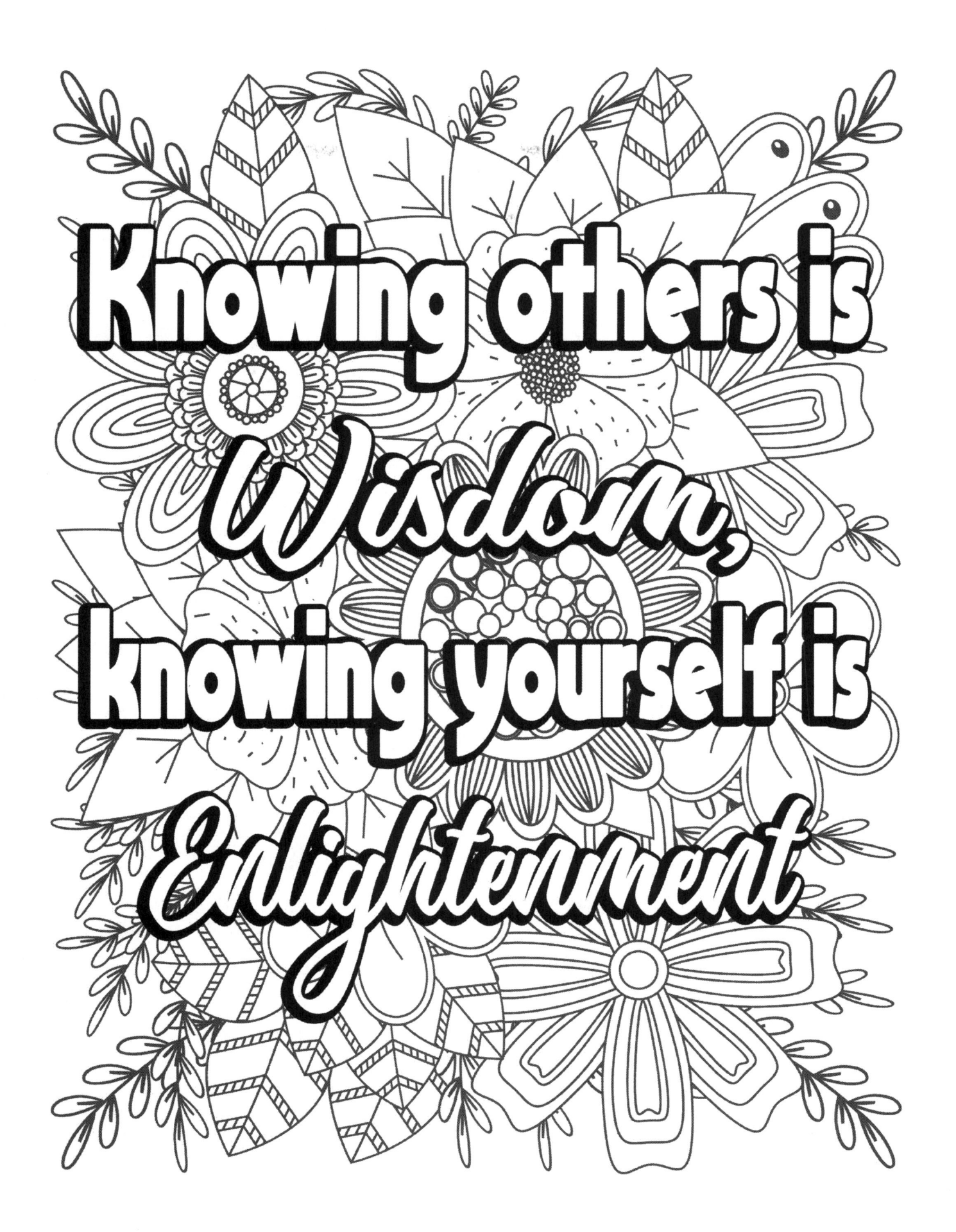

Knowing others is Wisdom, knowing yourself is Enlightenment

When you accept yourself, the whole world accepts you

Look, and it can't be seen. Listen, and it can't be heard. Reach, and it can't be grasped.

Hold on to the center.

The way of heaven is to help and not harm

Figure out the rhythm of life and live in harmony with it

He who is contented is rich.

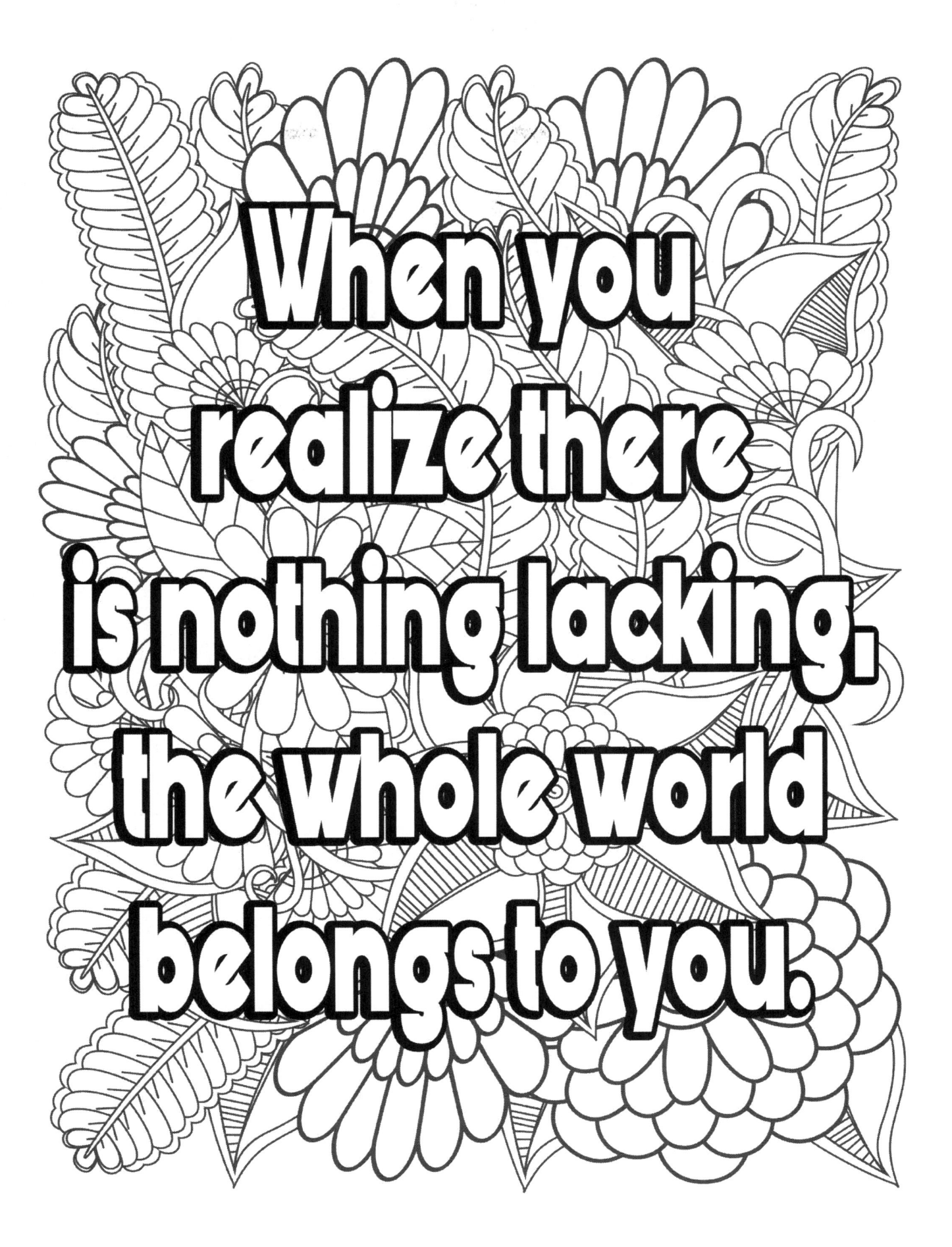

When you realize there is nothing lacking, the whole world belongs to you.

Mastering others is **STRENGTH.** Mastering yourself is **TRUE POWER**

The words of truth are always paradoxical.

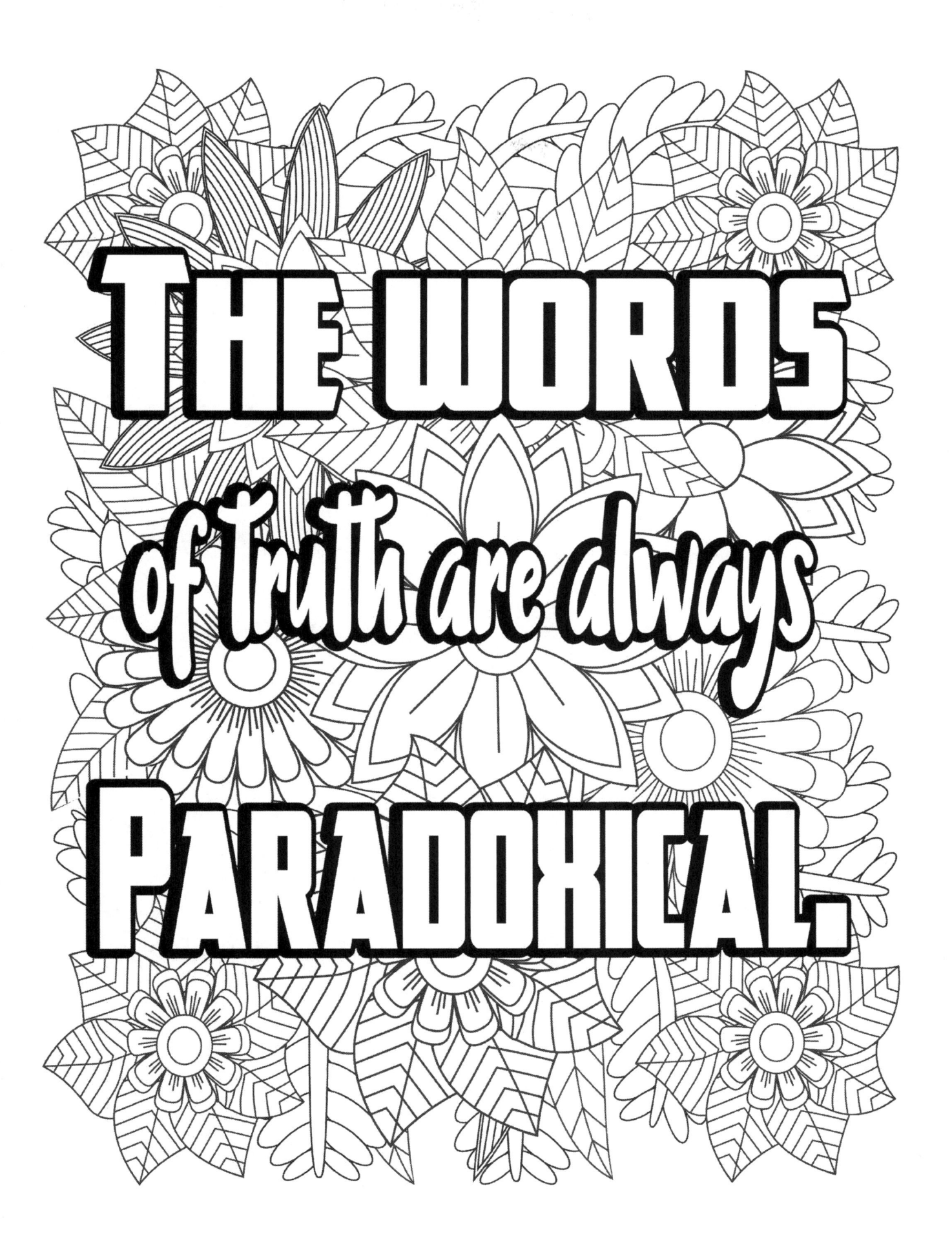

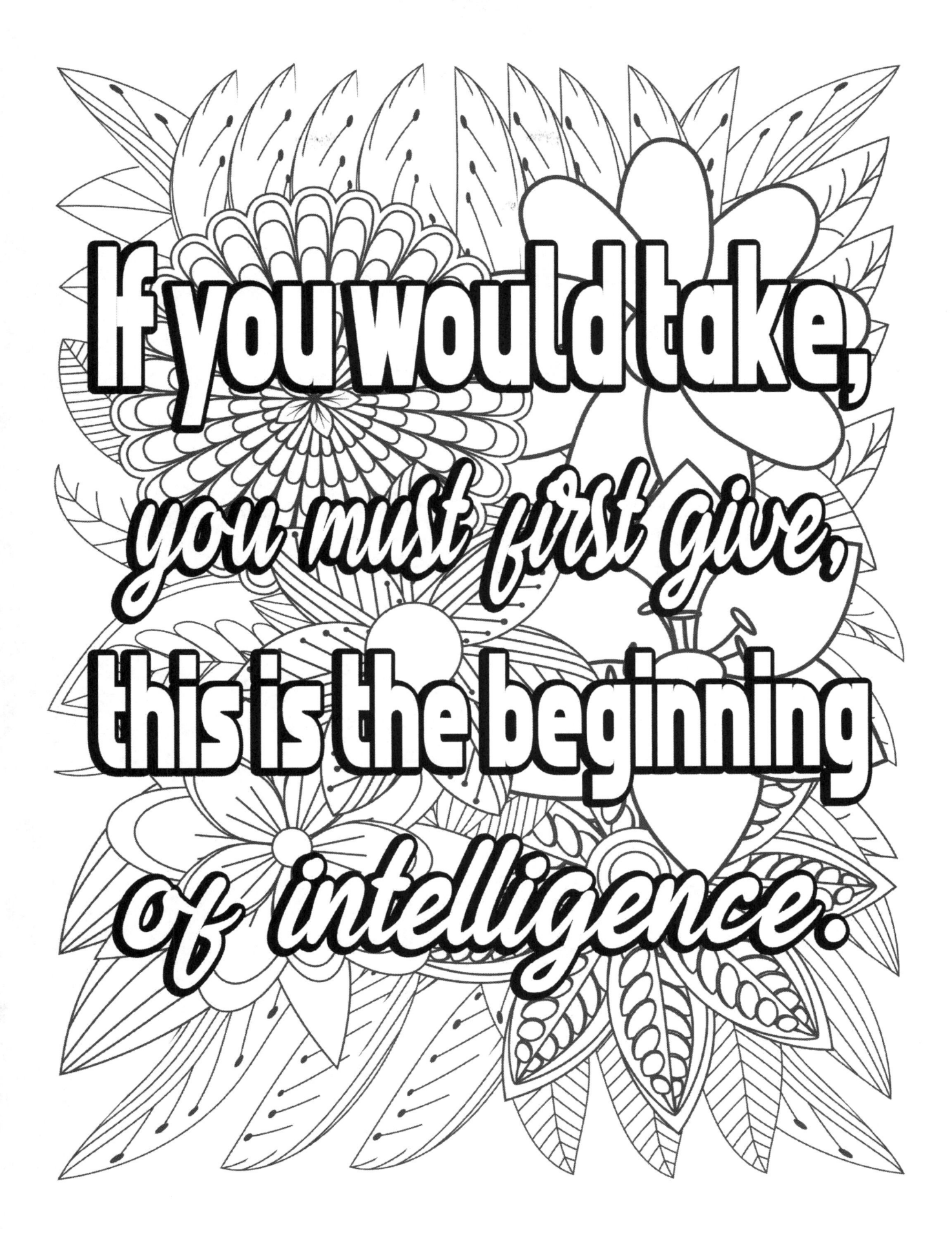

If you would take, you must first give, this is the beginning of intelligence.

Purity and stillness give the correct law to all under heaven.

The power of intuitive understanding will protect you from harm until the end of your days

With virtue and quietness one may conquer the world.

Wild winds never last all morning And fierce rains never last all day

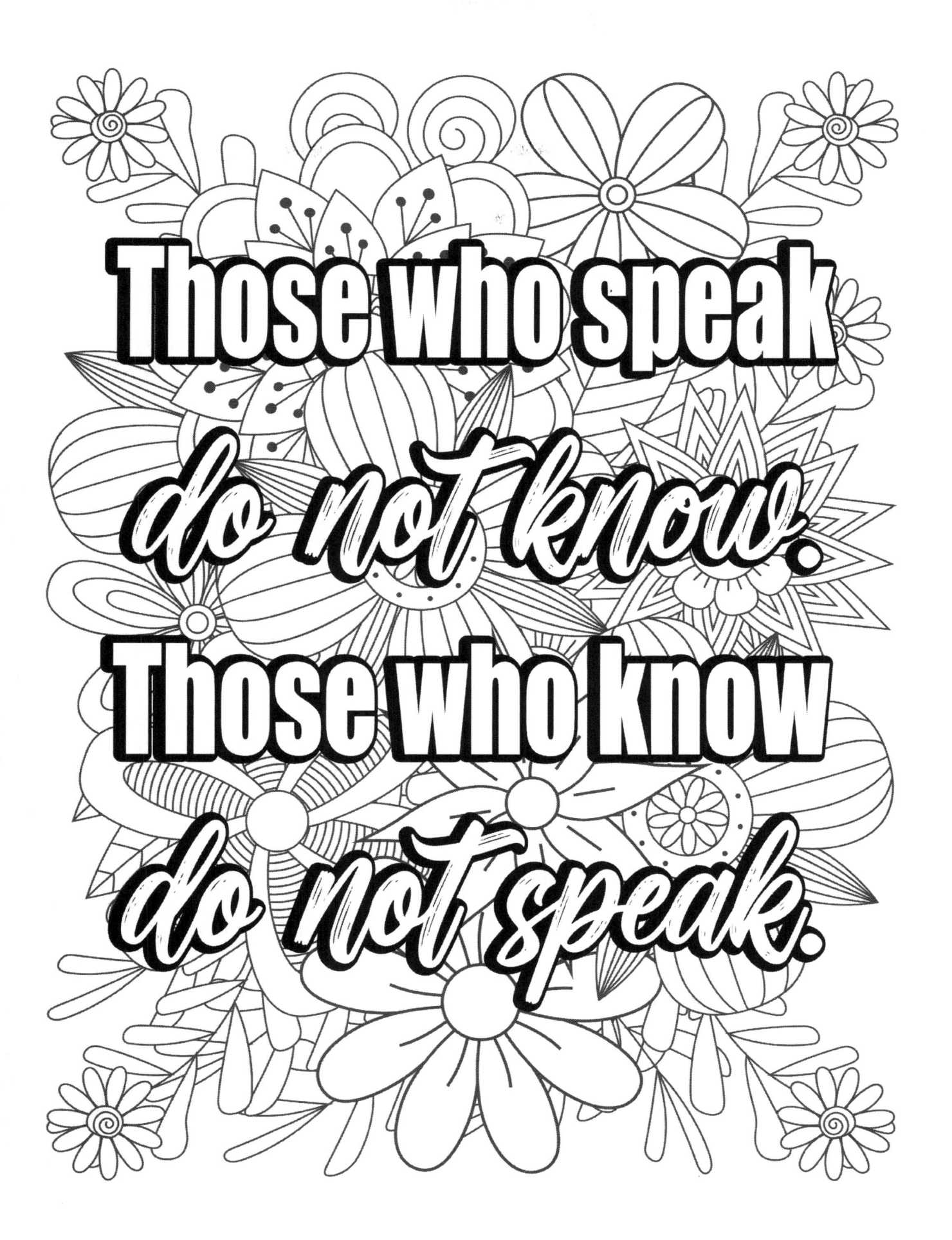

Those who speak do not know. Those who know do not speak.

Great Talents mature slowly.

TO RECOGNIZ *your insignificance* IS EMPOWERING.

ONE GAINS BY *losing and loses* BY GAINING

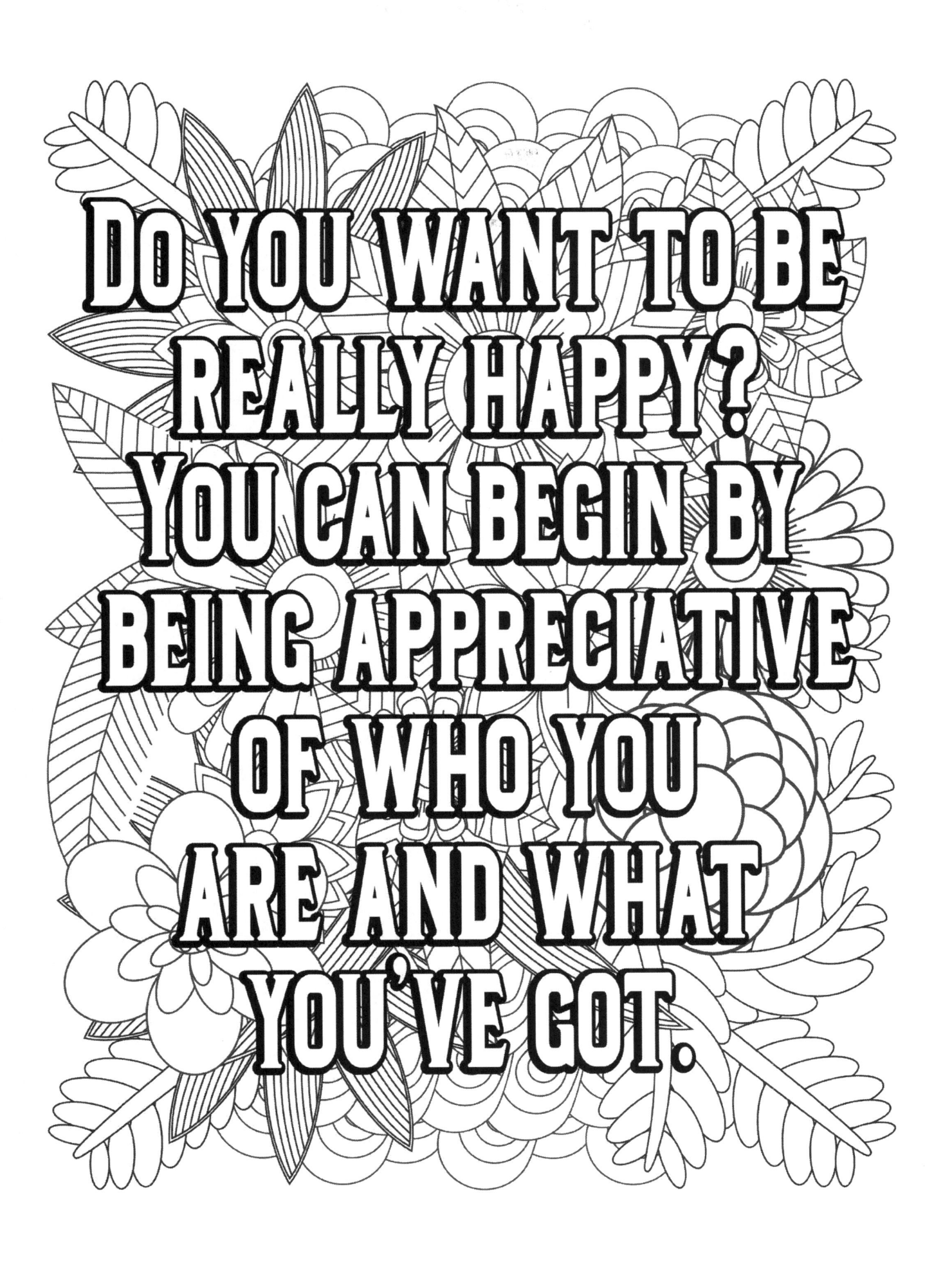

Do you want to be really happy? You can begin by being appreciative of who you are and what you've got.

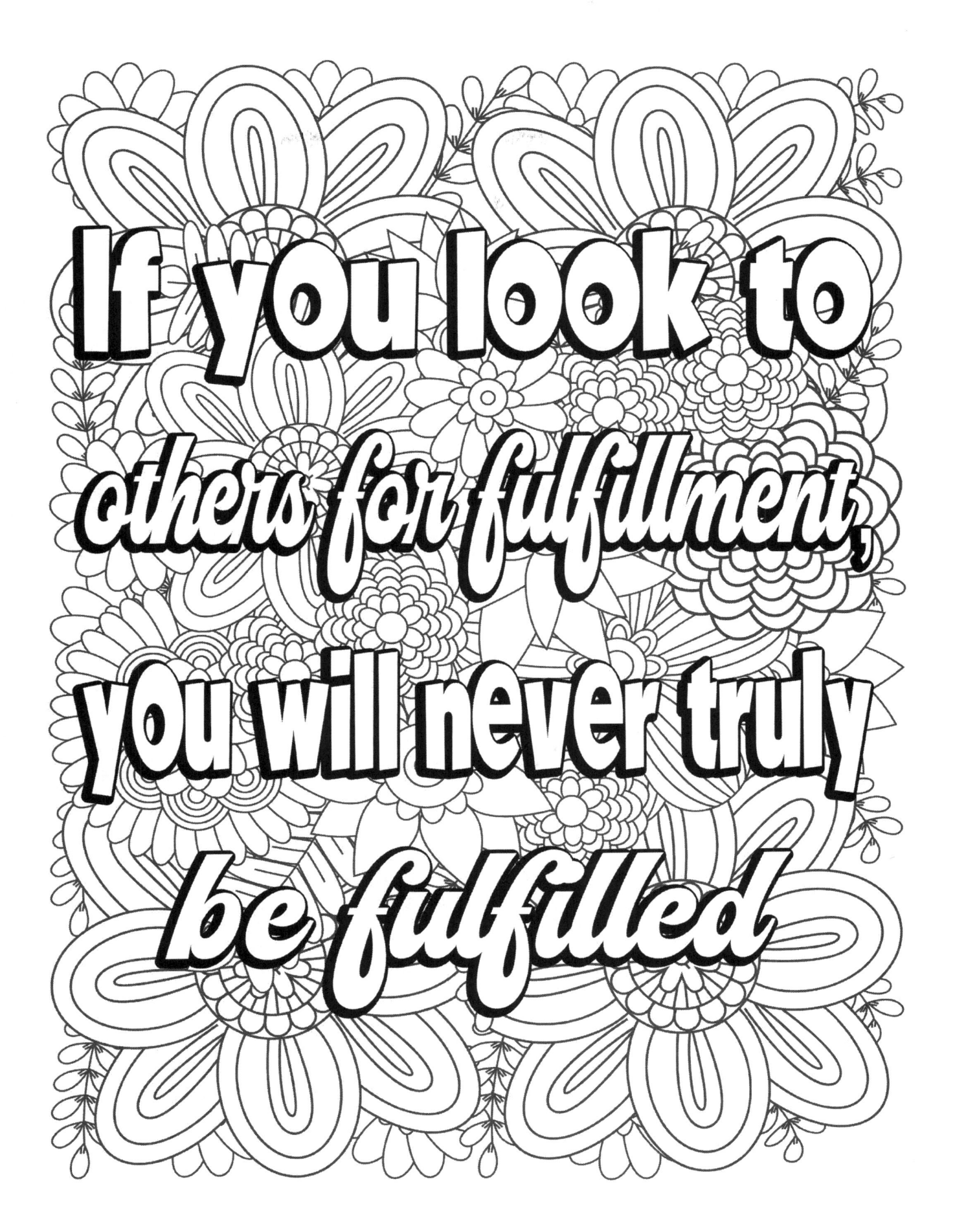

If you look to others for fulfillment, you will never truly be fulfilled

Thank You

FOR YOUR

Review

Please Share Your Feedback

We wanted to take a moment to express our sincere gratitude for using our Coloring Book. Your support means a lot to us.
If you had a positive experience with the book, we would be extremely grateful if you could take a few minutes to leave a review on the platform you purchased it from. Your feedback and thoughts about the book would be incredibly valuable for others who are interested in purchasing it and for us as authors. Your review will help spread the word and reach more people who love coloring.
Thank you again for your support.

Made in the USA
Columbia, SC
13 May 2024